snapshot·picture·library

CARS

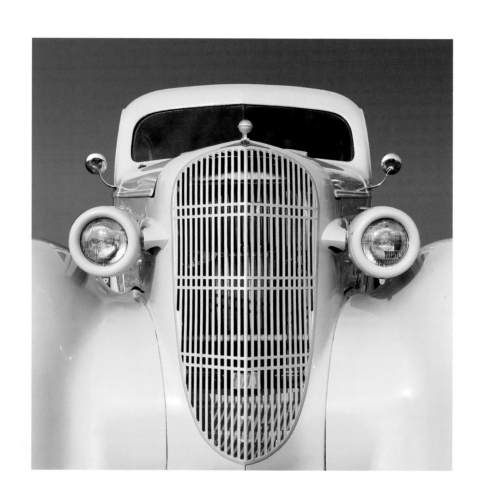

snapshot·picture·library

CARS

FOG CITY PRESS

Published by Fog City Press,
a division of Weldon Owen Inc.
415 Jackson Street
San Francisco, CA 94111 USA
www.weldonowen.com

WELDON OWEN INC.

Group Publisher, Bonnier Publishing Group John Owen
President, CEO Terry Newell
Senior VP, International Sales Stuart Laurence
VP, Sales and New Business Development Amy Kaneko
VP, Publisher Roger Shaw
Executive Editor Elizabeth Dougherty
Assistant Editor Sarah Gurman
Associate Creative Director Kelly Booth
Senior Designer William Mack
Production Director Chris Hemesath
Production Manager Michelle Duggan
Color Manager Teri Bell

A WELDON OWEN PRODUCTION
© 2009 Weldon Owen Inc.

Library of Congress Control Number: 2009924571

ISBN: 978-1-74089-882-9

10 9 8 7 6 5 4 3 2 1
2009 2010 2011 2012

Printed by Tien Wah Press in Singapore.

The first cars were made over a hundred years ago. They were slow, and few people had them.

Today cars are much faster, and most families use one or more. Some cars are designed for racing on tracks; others for driving around town. There are many kinds of cars in many different sizes and colors. What's your favorite car?

Early cars were noisy and could travel only short distances.

Classic American cars from the
late 1950s were large and shiny.
Many had fins at the back.

European
cars tend to
be smaller.
They work well
for driving in
crowded cities.

Sports cars, like these older models, seat only two. They are small and light to help them go fast.

"Muscle" cars have big engines and can go very fast. Unlike sports cars, muscle cars have back seats.

Luxury sports cars offer comfortable seats, but not a smooth ride. They're built to go fast and round corners quickly.

Carmakers are always working to improve the ways cars work and look. The doors on this one swing up.

Transporter
trucks deliver
cars to lots
to be sold.

Most cars are used to transport family members (including pets!) and all the things they need to bring with them.

Car mechanics help take care of cars. They have special lifting machines so they can fix things underneath.

On a sunny day,
it's fun to wash
your family's car.
But be prepared
to get wet!

If you don't have a car,
you can take a taxi!

Stretch limos aren't just for movie stars! People can hire them for special occasions like birthdays or weddings.

Flashing lights and a loud siren warn drivers that a police car is coming—fast!

Government cars have
special security features to
protect important people.

Sometimes everyone gets on
the road at the same time,
causing a traffic jam!

Some cars can drive over rocks and through mud because they have big wheels that al ... ve t ...

Dune buggies can drive over sand—along beaches or across deserts.

Some cars can drive over rocks and through mud because they have big wheels that all move together.

Dune buggies can drive over sand—along beaches or across deserts.

Stock cars look like normal cars—but they have powerful engines built for racing.

"Pro-street" cars
have engines made
for drag racing.

Racing cars stop
in the pit lanes
to have their tires
changed or their
fuel tanks filled.
Everyone works
fast to get the car
back into the race.

Formula One racing cars have "wings" on the front and back to help keep the cars on the track.

This very, very fast car was built by hand to break speed records. It races in a straight line only in flat areas where it doesn't have to turn any corners.

Small cars don't need much fuel. They are cheaper to run than larger cars.

Electric cars and hybrid cars are good for the environment. They use batteries to help cut down on exhaust fumes.

A few cars run on hydrogen. Maybe lots of cars will use this kind of fuel in the future.

Cars can go lots of places. Where would you like to go for a drive?

Model T Ford

In 1908, Ford Motor Company started to sell the Model T, nicknamed the "Tin Lizzie." By 1914, the company was making a Model T every 24 seconds.

Classic Cadillac

In the 1950s, the United States was manufacturing more cars than any other country. American cars, like this pink Cadillac, were modern and stylish.

Mini

The Mini was first made in 1959. Like lots of European cars, it's very small—perfect for driving in cities and very easy to park.

Sports car

Most sports cars, like this Lotus Elise, are low to the ground and have very powerful engines. Even though these cars are fast, they aren't designed for racing.

Smart car

The Smart car is half the size of most cars. Nicolas Hayek, who invented the Swatch watch, teamed up with Mercedes-Benz to build this car.

Taxi

Taxis are useful for getting around in big cities. A meter tracks how much the ride costs. Many cities have cabs with a distinct look, like this London taxi.

Government car

Governments use official cars with special security features, such as this presidential limousine, to transport important people.

Jeep

The Jeep was originally designed as a general-purpose—or "GP," which sounds like "jeep"—vehicle. Now, many people use them for fun adventures.

Dune buggy

An open dune buggy is called a sandrail. It can drive along beaches or across deserts. Some drivers compete in dune-buggy races on sandy tracks.

Race car

Race cars, like this Formula One car, are built for speed. Formula One teams make the cars; each has an open cockpit and the engine in the back.

Hybrid car

Some cars have an electric battery but can also run on gasoline. They are called hybrids because they use two types of fuel, switching automatically between them.

Hydrogen car

A few cars run on hydrogen fuel cells, which combine hydrogen and oxygen in a way that generates electricity to power the car.

ACKNOWLEDGMENTS

Weldon Owen would like to thank the following people for their assistance in the production of this book: Cynthia O'Brien, author and researcher; Tu Hoang designer; Ellen Dupont, project manager.

CREDITS

Key t=top; b=bottom; iSP=iStockphoto; SST=Shutterstock; COR=Corbis; GET=Getty Images; PA=PA Photos
Jacket SST; **inside flap** SST; **2** SST; **5** SST; **6** SST; **8**t iSP, b SST; **9** SST; **10** iSP; **11** iSP; **12**t iSP, b SST; **13** iSP; **14** SST; **15**t SST, b SST; **16** SST; **18** SST; **19**t,b SST; **20** SST; **22**t,b SST; **23** SST; **24** COR; **25**t SST, b SST; **26** SST; **27**t,b SST; **28** SST; **30** SST; **31** SST; **32** SST; **34**t,b SST; **35** SST; **36** SST; **37** SST; **38** SST; **39** SST; **40** SST; **41**t,b iSP; **42**t,b SST; **43** SST; **44** SST; **45** t,b SST; **46** SST; **48** SST; **50** iSP; **51**t,b SST; **52** SST; **54**t iSP, b SST; **55** SST; **56** GET; **57**t SST, b PA; **58** t PA, b SST; **59** SST; **60** SST; **64** SST.